D0426653

PHYSICAL SCIENCE PROJECTS
★ For Kids ★

A PROJECT GUIDE TO

CHEMISTRY

Claire O'Neal

Mitchell Lane

P.O. Box 196
Hockessin, Delaware 19707
Visit us on the web: www.mitchelllane.com
Comments? email us:
mitchelllane@mitchelllane.com

Mitchell Lane

PHYSICAL SCIENCE PROJECTS ★ for kids ★

A Project Guide to:

Electricity and Magnetism • Matter
Chemistry • Forces and Motion
Light and Optics • Sound

PUBLISHER'S NOTE: The facts on which the story in this book is based have been thoroughly researched. Documentation of such research can be found on page 44. While every possible effort has been made to ensure accuracy, the publisher will not assume liability for damages caused by inaccuracies in the data, and makes no warranty on the accuracy of the information contained herein.

To reflect current usage, we have chosen to use the secular era designations BCE ("before the common era") and CE ("of the common era") instead of the traditional designations BC ("before Christ") and AD (anno Domini, "in the year of the Lord").

The internet sites referenced herein were active as of the publication date. Due to the fleeting nature of some web sites, we cannot guarantee they will all be active when you are reading this book.

**Library of Congress
Cataloging-in-Publication Data applied for**

eBook ISBN: 9781612281100

Printing 1 2 3 4 5 6 7 8 9

PLB

CONTENTS

Introduction.. 4

What Does an Atom Look Like?................................ 6

Gumdrop Hydrocarbons 10

Chemical Reactions in Your Kitchen 14

Reaction Products 16

Hot or Cold.. 20

Is It an Acid or a Base?..................................... 23

Redox Reactions 27

    Fast Oxidation: Burning Oxygen 28

    Slow Oxidation: Rusting Steel Wool 30

Clean Your Mother's Silver 32

Metal Plating 35

Make Your Own Plastic 37

Breaking Bonds in Nature: Proteases....................... 40

Further Reading 44

    Books.. 44

    Works Consulted 44

    On the Internet 45

Glossary... 46

Index... 47

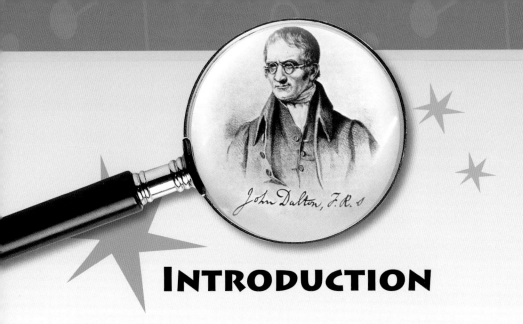

INTRODUCTION

Imagine the power of an **atom**! Atoms are so tiny that thousands can fit in a single speck of dust. But combine one type of atom with another, like ingredients in a recipe, and you can make an ocean of water, a spinning star, the DNA that makes us human, or a nuclear bomb. An atom may be puny, but a universe full of them holds enormous possibilities.

Hiding where no one could see it, the atom was only really discovered about 200 years ago. Over 2,000 years ago, Greek philosopher Democritus (460–370 BCE) thought that matter must be made of tiny particles that could not be divided. In his time, people laughed at him. His audience had a hard time believing anything they couldn't see. Shortly after that, Greek scientist Aristotle (384–322 BCE) proposed a theory that all of creation was made of earth, air, wind, and fire. Most people believed his theory until the nineteenth century.

John Dalton (1766–1844 CE) boldly suggested otherwise. Often known as the Father of the Atom, Dalton proposed that atoms of one **element** are all the same; and further, that two or more atoms could join, or **bond** together, to make **molecules**. Around the same time, Antoine Lavoisier (1743–1794) discovered that matter can be neither created nor destroyed—a physical law called the law of the **conservation of mass.** This law helped chemists understand that elements combine in predictable ways. For example, two hydrogen atoms (H) could join with one oxygen atom (O) to make water (H_2O).

By 2011, chemists had discovered 118 different elements. We know now that elements and molecules react with one another according to simple rules. Chemistry is the science that studies these rules—how elements interact, react, and combine, and especially how they affect life as we know it. The ground on which we walk is made from minerals—strong, stable compounds of elements created inside the earth. Cars and buses burn fuel, breaking the bonds in hydrocarbon molecules and converting that energy into motion. Nuclear power plants use energy from the natural breakdown of **radioactive** elements to electrify whole cities. When you eat, your stomach uses strong **acids** and enzymes—**proteins** that speed up chemical reactions—to break down food into the simpler elements your body needs to live.

Chemists aim to discover the secrets to nature's recipes, harnessing their power to work for us in new and exciting ways. Explore chemical reactions and more through the simple experiments and projects in this book.

Follow these rules for success and safety:

1. Ask **an adult** for permission before starting any experiment.
2. Read the instructions all the way through and make sure you understand them before beginning.
3. Have all materials and equipment you will need ready to go before you start.
4. Keep a special notebook to record your observations and thoughts as you perform the experiments.

Whether for a school project or just for fun, you'll learn to think like a chemist while using materials you probably already have at home. Let's get cooking!

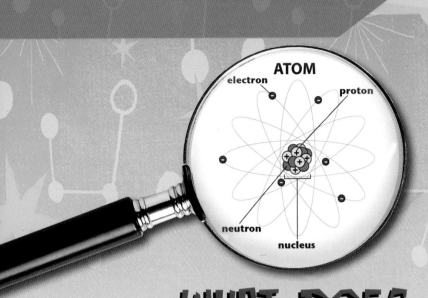

ATOM

electron

proton

neutron

nucleus

WHAT DOES AN ATOM LOOK LIKE?

If you think an atom is small, think about its parts! Three types of particles come together to make an atom—negatively charged **electrons,** positively charged **protons**, and **neutrons**, which have no charge (they are neutral). The number of protons in an atom, its **atomic number**, identifies which element it is. Electrons orbit the **nucleus**, where an atom's protons and neutrons are packed together. If a proton or a neutron were marble-sized, a tiny electron would be only the size of a grain of sand.

Danish physicist Niels Bohr (1885–1962) introduced a "solar system" model of the atom in 1917. In it, electrons occupy special 3-D orbits, or shells, around a nucleus. Each shell has space for a certain number of electrons (see the table on page 7). The shells increase in number and size as they get farther from the nucleus. Although scientists work with an updated view of atomic structure, Bohr's model remains popular in chemistry classrooms because it helps to explain how elements behave chemically.

To see an atom up close, build your own Bohr model.

Shell Number	Maximum Number of Electrons in Outer Shell	Elements
1	2	Hydrogen, Helium
2	8	Lithium, Beryllium, Boron, Carbon, Nitrogen, Oxygen, Fluorine, Neon
3	18	Sodium, Magnesium, Aluminum, Silicon, Phoshorus, Sulfur, Chlorine, Argon

MATERIALS

- periodic table of the elements (see page 8)
- modeling clay in three colors
- hot glue gun
- toothpicks
- fake spider webs of different colors (optional; available from craft stores)
- bamboo skewers
- scissors

INSTRUCTIONS

1. Choose an element from the periodic table. What is its atomic number?
2. Make balls the size of large marbles out of two colors of modeling clay to represent protons (color A) and neutrons (color B). Use the mass number to determine how many clay protons and neutrons to make. For nitrogen, for example, make 7 balls of each color.
3. Make tiny balls from color C to represent electrons. Use the same number of electrons as protons to make a neutral atom. How many shells will you need to contain your electrons?
4. With **an adult's** help, use a hot glue gun to glue the protons and neutrons together into a packed ball-shaped nucleus, arranging the particles evenly throughout.
5. To make the first electron shell, sink two toothpicks evenly into the clay. Mount electrons onto the toothpick tips. If you like, drape fake spider webs along the tips to illustrate the three-dimensional electron shell. Your two electrons, fixed in space, represent an atomic

Periodic Table of the Elements

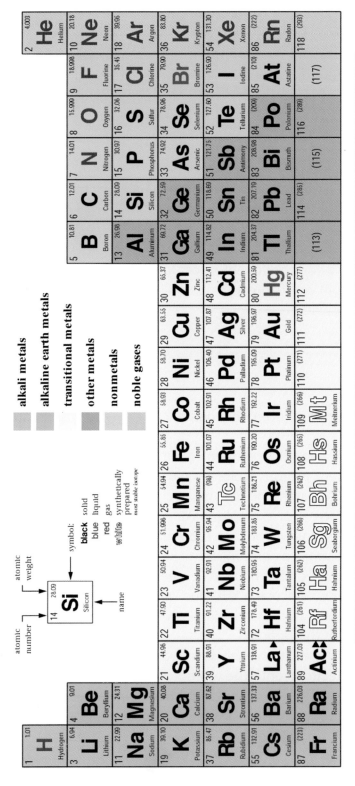

From clay to atoms! An easy way for you to see their structure.

snapshot; electrons move constantly and randomly within their shell.

6. If your element needs a second electron shell, snip four bamboo skewers in half with scissors. Insert each skewer evenly into the nucleus and mount electrons on the exposed tips. If you like, drape a different colored spider web over the electrons.

7. If your element needs a third electron shell, repeat step 6, but with whole bamboo skewers.

8. Study your atom. The number of electrons in its outermost shell determines how it will react with other atoms. Atoms with a mostly full outer shell react to gain electrons and complete the shell; atoms with a mostly empty outer shell react to empty it. How many does yours have in its outer shell? Will your atom be more likely to attract electrons or give them away?

Take it further: Research your atom. Are there any **isotopes**, or varieties with different numbers of neutrons? Build atoms of different elements to see how they compare in size and in the number of electrons in their outer shells.

GUMDROP HYDROCARBONS

Carbon atoms work together to make the chemistry of life. Carbon has 6 electrons—2 in the first shell and 4 in the second. Since its outer shell is half full (4 out of 8), each carbon atom seeks out 4 covalent bonds—bonds where electrons are shared equally between atoms. Carbon's ability to share electrons attracts hydrogen, oxygen, nitrogen, and other carbon atoms to make incredibly stable molecules, such as sugars, proteins, and fats.

Hydrogen and carbon combine to make long, energy-rich chains called hydrocarbons. These compounds are found in the fats we eat as well as in gasoline. Hydrocarbon chains take very different shapes depending on the type of bonds formed through the carbon backbone. Alkanes use single bonds between carbons and have the most flexible chains; they pack together easily to form a solid at room temperature. You probably eat alkanes every day, as butter and fats found in meats. They are known as saturated fats because they are "saturated"—completely full of hydrogen atoms. Unsaturated fats from plants, such as olive oil and canola oil, are alkenes. Alkenes have at least one carbon-carbon double bond, which kinks the chain and makes it less able to pack tightly. Alkenes are often liquid at room temperature. Rare in

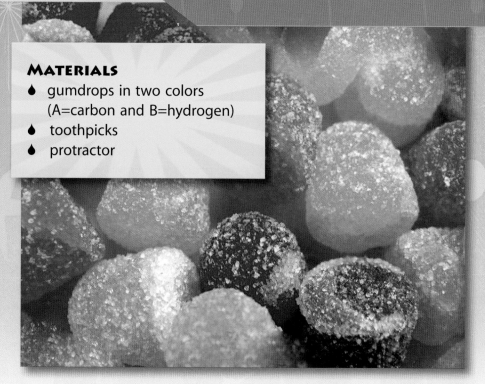

MATERIALS

- gumdrops in two colors
  (A=carbon and B=hydrogen)
- toothpicks
- protractor

nature are alkynes, whose triple bond between carbon atoms makes them unstable. Acetylene gas is an alkyne used in welding torches.

Take a closer look at how carbon makes its bonds by building gumdrop models of hydrocarbon atoms.

A. Each carbon must have four bonds.

Single bonds measure 109 degrees apart from each other, making a tetrahedron around the bonded carbon.

Double bonds make a flat plane, where angles between the bonds measure 120 degrees.

Triple bonds measure 180 degrees apart from the single bond, making a straight line.

B. Each hydrogen atom must have only one bond.

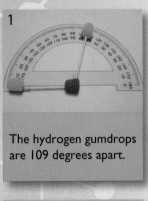

1

The hydrogen gumdrops are 109 degrees apart.

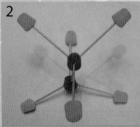

2

The carbon atoms bond to each other and to 3 hydrogen atoms.

3

Since these are all single bonds, the angle is still 109 degrees.

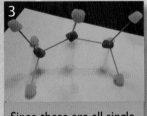

4

Make the double bond first. Then add hydrogen atoms at 120 degrees.

1. Build methane (CH_4), a greenhouse gas and the major component of natural gas. Mount a hydrogen gumdrop on one end of a toothpick. Insert the free toothpick end into the carbon gumdrop. Repeat three more times, following the bond angle rules for alkanes, until four hydrogen gumdrops are toothpick-bonded to the same carbon gumdrop. Methane makes a tetrahedron (a shape with four faces).

2. Ethane (C_2H_6) is also found in natural gas. Using toothpicks, bond two carbon gumdrops together to make the carbon backbone. Now add hydrogen gumdrops, as you did for methane. You should find that you need 3 hydrogen atoms for every carbon atom to make this molecule.

3. Propane (C_3H_8) is a fuel used in heating and cooking. Make the carbon backbone by bonding three carbon atoms together. Now add hydrogen gumdrops to fill out the required number of bonds to each carbon. You should find that the middle carbon atoms bond with 2 hydrogen atoms, while the end carbon atoms bond with 3 hydrogen atoms.

4. Build a simple alkene, such as ethylene (C_2H_4). Join two carbon gumdrops using two toothpicks parallel to each other. Bond two hydrogen gumdrops to each carbon gumdrop, making a flat molecule.

5. Build acetylene, an alkyne (C_2H_2). Join two carbon gumdrops with three parallel toothpicks. Bond one hydrogen gumdrop to each carbon, making a straight line of gumdrop atoms.

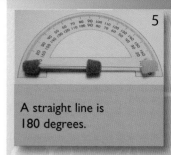

A straight line is 180 degrees.

6. Build longer alkanes and alkenes. Pentane (C_5H_{12}) is the shortest hydrocarbon that exists as a liquid at room temperature. Create shapes—like triangles, squares, circles, or branches—just by altering the connections of the carbon backbone. Research longer hydrocarbons to find some that are solid at room temperature. Can you build a model to explain why?

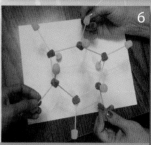

A circle of 6 carbon atoms, known as cyclohexane, is particularly stable in nature.

Carbon (red gumdrops) bonds to hydrogen (white gumdrops) in many different ways. Make a tasty model yourself!

CHEMICAL REACTIONS IN YOUR KITCHEN

Under just the right conditions, one molecule plus another molecule can make something entirely new through a chemical **reaction.** Chemical equations are useful for describing reactions. The **reactants,** or starting materials, are listed on the left side, while the products are listed on the right. Instead of an equal sign, chemists use an arrow that means "yields." The number of atoms for each type of element remains the same on both sides of the equation, but how they are grouped— the molecules—changes. For example, the reaction between two household substances, baking soda and vinegar, is written like this:

$$C_2H_4O_2 + NaHCO_3 \rightarrow H_2CO_3 + NaC_2H_3O_2$$

Like a chemical sentence, this reaction equation reads: "acetic acid (vinegar) and sodium bicarbonate (baking soda) yields carbonic acid and sodium acetate." A simpler way to describe the reaction, however, is to write it this way:

$$CH_3COOH + NaHCO_3 \rightarrow HHCO_3 + CH_3COONa$$

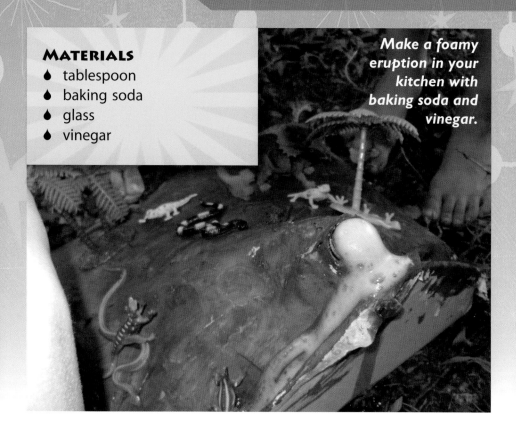

Make a foamy eruption in your kitchen with baking soda and vinegar.

The **cations** (in red)—hydrogen and sodium—and **anions** (in blue)—acetate and bicarbonate—switch partners. Check this reaction out for yourself!

INSTRUCTIONS

1. Add a few tablespoons of baking soda to a glass.
2. Pour vinegar straight from the bottle and watch the reaction. What is happening?
3. Now that you've tried the reaction, be more precise. For example, how much vinegar do you need to bubble away 1 tablespoon of baking soda?

Take it further: The baking soda–vinegar reaction is a favorite to use in making homemade volcanoes. Sculpt a volcano out of modeling clay or papier-mâché with a bottle or glass in the center. Pour baking soda and vinegar into the bottle or glass to make your volcano erupt.

REACTION PRODUCTS

In the baking soda–vinegar reaction, what happens to the products? You can't see sodium or acetate, but they haven't disappeared. The law of conservation of mass states that matter—such as sodium and acetate—cannot be created or destroyed. These cations and anions **dissolved** in the water. Carbonic acid, however, makes a very visible escape. It breaks down quickly to make water and carbon dioxide gas. The gas is released as bubbles, which tells you the reaction is working.

$$H_2CO_3 \longrightarrow CO_2 \text{ (gas)} + H_2O \text{ (liquid)}$$

Other reactions can yield products that do not dissolve in water. They drop to the floor of the reaction container as a solid **precipitate**. You can create a precipitate by reacting two different common household chemicals, Epsom salts and ammonia.

MATERIALS

- 2 one-cup glass jars
- ¼ cup water
- 1 teaspoon Epsom salts (magnesium sulfate)
- spoon
- household ammonia (ammonium hydroxide)
- coffee filter
- magnifying glass
- ½ teaspoon alum (aluminum sulfate) (found in the grocery store's spice section)
- vinegar
- eyedropper

$$MgSO_4 + 2\,NH_4OH \longrightarrow (NH_4)_2SO_4 + Mg(OH)_2$$

This reaction equation reads: "magnesium sulfate (Epsom salts, a solid) and ammonium hydroxide (ammonia, in **solution**) yields ammonium sulfate (in solution) and magnesium hydroxide (a solid).

Be sure to carry out your reaction in a well-ventilated area, as ammonia has very strong fumes.

INSTRUCTIONS

1. Add the water to one glass jar. Add the Epsom salts and stir to dissolve.
2. Add 2 teaspoons ammonia to the Epsom salt solution without stirring.
3. Watch the reaction. During this quiet reaction, a jelly-like substance forms at the top of the liquid. Over time, it will collect at the bottom of the jar. This gel is magnesium hydroxide, also known as milk of magnesia.
4. Set a coffee filter atop the second jar. Pour the contents of the first jar through the filter so that the solution passes into the clean jar

Epsom salts and ammonia react to form magnesium hydroxide.

and the white precipitate (the gel) collects on the filter. Leave the second jar in a warm place for a day or so.

5. Once all the water evaporates, you should see crystals of pure ammonium sulfate, though you may need a magnifying glass to see them. This chemical is used to purify public water supplies.

6. Repeat steps 1-5 using ½ teaspoon of alum in place of magnesium sulfate to create a different precipitate via the following reaction:

Aluminum sulfate + ammonia → **ammonium sulfate + aluminum hydroxide**
     (solution)   (solution)   (solution)   (solid)

7. Label the two coffee filters and compare the two precipitates you made side by side. What do they look like? Are they grainy? Colored? Can you tell if one reaction created more precipitate than the other?

8. Place each filter on a clean plate. Add a little vinegar, one drop at a time, to the magnesium hydroxide on the filter. The vinegar will react with the magnesium hydroxide to make magnesium acetate. The reaction happens like this:

$$Mg(OH)_2 + 2\ CH_3COOH \rightarrow Mg(CH_3COO)_2 + 2\ HOH$$

$$\text{(solid)}\quad\text{(solution)}\qquad\qquad\text{(solution)}\quad\text{(liquid)}$$

Magnesium hydroxide + acetic acid $\rightarrow$ magnesium acetate + water

This type of reaction is called an acid-**base** reaction. Magnesium hydroxide is a base that reacts with vinegar, an acid. All acid-base reactions form water and a salt that dissolves in the water. The magnesium hydroxide (a base) reacts with vinegar (an acid) to yield water and magnesium acetate (a salt that dissolves in water). Add vinegar to the aluminum hydroxide you made to see a similar reaction.

Take it further: Antacids such as Maalox and Mylanta contain magnesium hydroxide and/or aluminum hydroxide, just like the precipitates you made. Crumble up some antacids in a cup and add vinegar. These products react with stomach acid—like the vinegar—to create water and a soluble salt.

The white precipitate lets you know your reaction worked!

HOT OR COLD

Temperature plays an important role in chemical reactions. Temperature is actually a measure of energy—how quickly atoms are moving and rubbing against each other to create heat. At hot temperatures, atoms move faster and with higher energy, making it more likely that two reacting particles will collide. At cold temperatures, atoms move slowly and with lower energy, decreasing their chances for interaction.

Let's see how temperature affects the baking soda and vinegar reaction.

MATERIALS

- 3 empty, narrow-neck plastic bottles
- funnel
- baking soda
- marker
- Pyrex (heat-proof) measuring cup
- vinegar
- thermometer
- 3 balloons
- plastic wrap
- a friend
- stopwatch
- fabric measuring tape
- refrigerator
- microwave
- oven mitts

Be ready to attach the balloon. This reaction goes fast!

INSTRUCTIONS

1. Using a funnel, pour 1 tablespoon baking soda into each of the three bottles. With the marker, label the first bottle ROOM TEMPERATURE, the second bottle COLD, and the third bottle HOT.

2. Measure ½ cup vinegar and record its temperature. Have a balloon ready to go; arm your friend with a stopwatch. Quickly pour the cup of vinegar into the room-temperature bottle, stretch the opening of the balloon over the bottle's mouth, and have your friend start the stopwatch.

    What is happening in the bottle? What is happening to the balloon? Shake the bottle from time to time to help the baking soda react as completely as possible. Stop the stopwatch when the reaction no longer makes bubbles. Measure around the balloon at its widest point.

Carbon dioxide from the reaction inflates the balloon, like magic!

3. Pour ½ cup of fresh vinegar into the Pyrex measuring cup. Cover the cup with plastic wrap and set it in a refrigerator for at least two hours. Repeat the procedure in step 2.
4. Pour ½ cup of fresh vinegar into the Pyrex cup. This time, microwave the cup of vinegar for 30 seconds. Use caution, as the vinegar will be near boiling. Using oven mitts, repeat the procedure in step 2.
5. Compare the three reactions. Which was fastest and which was slowest? How do the final diameters of the balloons compare? Were they different? Why or why not?

Take it further: What happens if you use different amounts of the baking soda, vinegar, or both?

IS IT AN ACID OR A BASE?

Most of the liquids you use every day are solutions of compounds dissolved in water. Whether for drinking or cleaning, they all are either acids, bases, or neutral. How acidic or basic a solution is, its **pH**, is measured on a scale of 0 to 14, with 7.0 being neutral. When added to water, acids (pH < 7.0) release positive **ions,** usually H^+ (hydrogen ions), which lowers the pH of the solution. Bases (pH > 7.0) raise the pH of the solution by releasing negative ions, usually hydroxide (OH^-), into the water.

Acidic liquids like lemon juice (pH 2.3) and orange juice (pH 3.5) taste tart and dry. Basic liquids taste soapy or bitter. Baking soda solution, sometimes used to calm an upset stomach (pH 8.0), is a base. Bases such as bleach make great cleaners, though you certainly would not want to drink them!

Want to find out more about the pH of solutions in your house? Make a pH indicator from red cabbage or turmeric, a yellow spice, to test samples and see for yourself.

Red Cabbage Indicator

Red cabbage contains anthocyanin, a purplish-red plant pigment that changes color based on the pH of its environment. To obtain a strong anthocyanin solution, you will need:

MATERIALS
- small head of red cabbage
- knife and cutting board
- **an adult**
- distilled water
- stockpot with lid
- stove
- pot holders
- colander
- sink
- large bowl
- 1-quart glass jar with screw-top lid

Get the best results with distilled water, which is purer than tap water.

INSTRUCTIONS

1. **With an adult's help**, chop the red cabbage into small pieces. Add the pieces to a stockpot. Add enough distilled water to just cover the cabbage.
2. **With an adult's help**, place the stockpot on a burner. Put the lid on the pot and heat the cabbage to boiling. Turn the heat to medium and continue to boil the cabbage, covered, for 30 minutes. Turn off the burner and allow the cabbage to sit on the stove until cool enough to handle.

Put a bowl under the colander to catch the cabbage juice. You'll need it later!

3. Place the colander over a large bowl in the sink. Use pot holders to carry the stockpot to the sink, and carefully pour the boiled cabbage into the colander. Collect the dark bluish-purple liquid that boiled off in the large bowl underneath. Use the cabbage for other purposes (eat it and make your mom proud!), but save the liquid. It is the pH indicator. Keep the indicator in a glass jar in the refrigerator until needed.

4. You can use the indicator at full strength, or you can dilute it by half using distilled water. Add the indicator one drop at a time to a solution you want to test until you see a change in color. Match the color with the chart below to find out the pH of your substance:

pH 2 → red
pH 4 → purple
pH 6 → violet
pH 8 → blue
pH 10 → green
pH 12 → greenish yellow

Cabbage juice indicator turns a glass of vinegar pink. It must be an acid!

Turmeric Indicator

MATERIALS
- turmeric powder
- rubbing alcohol
- spoon
- glass jar with screw-top lid

INSTRUCTIONS
1. Combine ½ teaspoon turmeric powder with ½ cup rubbing alcohol and stir until dissolved. Keep the indicator in a small glass jar in the refrigerator until ready to use.
2. Add the turmeric indicator one drop at a time to the solution you want to test. If the solution has a pH greater than 8.6, the indicator will turn from yellow to a strong red color.

Make Indicator Paper
Add a pH indicator solution to a shallow bowl or dish. Drag coffee filters, cut into 1-inch strips, through the liquid. Set the wet strips on a baking sheet to dry. To use, dip the dry strips into test solutions, or drop test solutions onto the strips. Store the strips in a dry, closed container.

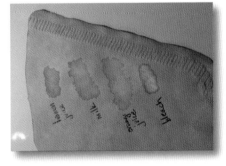

Experiment!
Use your indicators to test the pH of common household liquids (tap water, rainwater, juice, milk, tea, brewed coffee, vinegar, ammonia, bleach, window cleaner), comparing them to the pH of distilled water, which should be neutral at pH 7.0. Make solutions of common powders, such as baking soda, baking powder, or powdered cleansers, by dissolving 1 tablespoon powder in 1 cup distilled water.

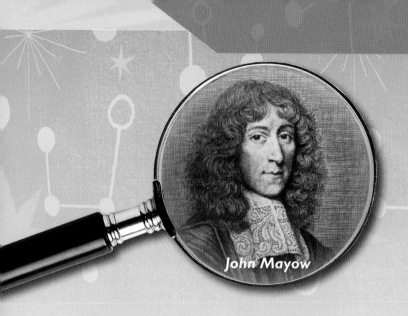

John Mayow

REDOX REACTIONS

Special reactions, called **redox** reactions, occur when electrons move from one reaction partner to another. *Redox* is short for "reduction-oxidation." In redox reactions, one substance gives up electrons (or is **oxidized**) to the other substance involved. The second substance gains electrons (or is **reduced**).

The reaction gets its name from the element oxygen. Oxygen has six electrons in its outer shell. Because it needs only two more for the shell to be full, oxygen strongly attracts electrons. In the heat of a fire, oxygen rapidly gains electrons from wood, using the wood's starches to make carbon dioxide. Another oxidation process, rusting, happens slowly, as oxygen from the air gains electrons from iron. Let's take a look at both fast and slow oxidation.

Fast Oxidation: Burning Oxygen

People believed that air was a pure element for thousands of years, until John Mayow (1641–1679) proved them wrong. In a classic experiment, Mayow burned a candle in a water-sealed jar. The flame consumed something in the air, creating a vacuum that sucked water into the jar. Before water could fill the jar, however, the flame died. Mayow showed what this must mean: that only part of the air served as fuel for the fire and, when the fuel ran out, so did the flame.

Mayow believed that the candle burned "nitro-aerial spirit." A century later, Joseph Priestley (1733–1804) discovered that the fuel the fire consumed was actually oxygen. Scientists today know that air contains 78 percent nitrogen, 21 percent oxygen, and trace amounts of other gases, mainly argon and carbon dioxide. Under the right conditions, oxygen in the air reacts violently with carbon-containing materials such as coal, wood, or natural gas. The following equation shows how this happens with propane:

$$C_3H_8 + 5O \rightarrow 3CO_2 + 4H_2O$$
$$\text{(propane)} + \text{(oxygen)} \rightarrow \text{(carbon dioxide)} + \text{(water)} + \text{heat}$$

This reaction gives off extreme amounts of heat, which we see as fire. The reaction—and the fire—continues until one of the reactants runs out. Repeat Mayow's experiment and see for yourself!

MATERIALS
- birthday candle
- cereal bowl
- clay
- water
- drinking glass
- permanent or waterproof marker
- matches
- **an adult**

INSTRUCTIONS

1. Stand a birthday candle upright in the bottom of a cereal bowl. Mold clay around the base of the candle to hold it in place.
2. Add water to the bowl so that it is about ¾ full.

When the candle goes out, the water moves in. Amaze your friends and family with this neat project!

3. Turn the glass upside down and cover the candle and clay with it, resting the mouth of the glass at the bottom of the bowl. Note the level of water in the glass with the waterproof marker.
4. Remove the glass and, with **an adult's** help, light the candle. Let it burn for a few seconds, then replace the glass.
5. Watch the level of water in the glass. When the flame goes out, mark the new level of water in the jar.

As the oxygen in the glass was consumed, the air inside the glass heated up and took up less space. Water moved into the glass to fill that space.

Take it further: Repeat the experiment using jars of different sizes and shapes. How do narrow-bottomed jars or curvy vases, for example, compare with cylindrical ones?

Slow Oxidation: Rusting Steel Wool

Iron is strong, but iron oxide (rust) is brittle and crumbles. Oxygen in the air rusts iron according to this chemical equation:

$$4 \text{ Fe} + 3 \text{ O}_2 \rightarrow 2 \text{ Fe}_2\text{O}_3$$
$$\text{iron} + \text{oxygen} \rightarrow \text{iron oxide}$$

You've seen this reaction in action on old cars. The slight acidity of rainwater slowly strips electrons away from the iron atoms in the cars' steel, creating iron cations that interact with oxygen in the air to form rust. In your house, you can speed up this effect by dunking steel wool in water or vinegar. Which will make the steel wool rust fastest—plain water, salt water, or vinegar?

MATERIALS
- 4 glass quart jars with screw-top lids
- clean steel wool, fresh from the package
- vinegar
- water
- salt
- permanent marker

Which will rust
the steel wool
fastest?

INSTRUCTIONS

1. Tear a wad of steel wool into four equal pieces. Place each piece in a glass jar.
2. Label one jar VINEGAR. Add enough vinegar to this jar to cover the steel wool.
3. To two jars, add enough water to cover the steel wool.
4. Label one jar SALT WATER. Add ¼ cup salt to the jar and stir until dissolved.
5. Leave the steel wool in the fourth jar uncovered. This will be your control.
6. Examine the jars every 15 minutes for 2 hours, and then twice daily for 3 days. Record your observations. Which liquid made the steel wool rust fastest?

Take it further: Try this reaction with clean pennies or copper strips to create copper oxide. Unlike rust, which destroys iron by making it brittle, the green residue of copper oxide forms a protective coating on the copper.

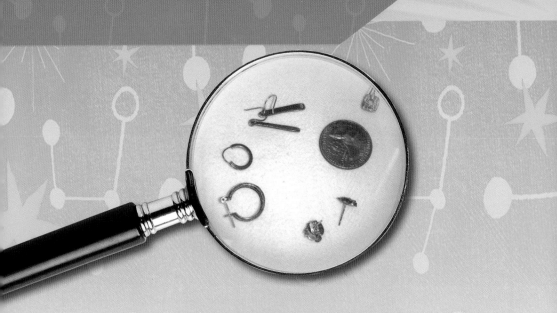

CLEAN YOUR MOTHER'S SILVER

Silver oxidizes over time by reacting with small amounts of sulfur in air or water, turning to the black compound silver sulfide. If silver could just find a source of free electrons, it could shed that ugly skin and gleam again. Luckily, you have an electron source in your cabinets already—aluminum foil. Tarnished silver attracts electrons from aluminum to make itself pure once more, tossing off its sulfide group onto the foil. The reaction looks like this:

$$3\ Ag_2S + 2\ Al \rightarrow 6\ Ag + Al_2S_3$$
$$\text{(silver sulfide) + (aluminum)} \rightarrow \text{(silver) + (aluminum sulfide)}$$

With your mother's permission, give her old, tarnished silver a hot salty bath to help those electrons flow, and her jewelry or silverware will look as good as new!

Tarnish washes right off the silver in this hot electron bath.

MATERIALS

- old, tarnished silver jewelry or cutlery
- digital camera
- 3 Pyrex baking dishes
- aluminum foil
- baking soda
- tablespoon
- 4-cup measuring cup
- water
- microwave
- oven mitts
- **an adult**
- dish towel

INSTRUCTIONS

1. Lay out the silver pieces you want to clean. Take photos of tarnished areas with the digital camera. Divide the pieces into three groups.
2. Label one baking dish ALUMINUM ONLY. Tear a piece of aluminum foil large enough to line its bottom and place one group of tarnished pieces on top. Label the second dish BAKING SODA ONLY. Place one group of tarnished pieces in the dish and sprinkle 3 tablespoons of baking soda over them. Label the third dish ALUMINUM + BAKING SODA. Line the bottom of this dish with aluminum foil, place the third group of tarnished pieces on top, and sprinkle 3 tablespoons of baking soda over them.

3. Fill the measuring cup with 4 cups of water. Microwave the cup on high power for 4 minutes or until boiling. With oven mitts and **an adult's** help, remove the hot cup from the microwave.

4. Pour the hot water slowly into the first dish. Watch the silver pieces and take notes.

5. Repeat steps 3 and 4 with the two remaining dishes. You may have to stir slightly to help the baking soda dissolve.

6. Remove the silver pieces from one dish at a time, rinse them under running water, and dry them with a dish towel. Be sure to keep the three groups separate. Take photos and compare them to those in step 1.

7. Compare the silver pieces between the three groups. Immersing aluminum foil in hot water is not enough to strip electrons from the aluminum (group 1), and a hot baking soda solution alone can't provide electrons for the silver either (group 2). But when the aluminum foil is immersed in a hot baking soda bath, the dissolved baking soda ions provide an ideal environment for electrons to jump out of the aluminum foil. Did you know you had created electron soup?

8. Inspect the aluminum foil in dishes 1 and 3. Does it look intact, or are there crumbly or less shiny spots where aluminum sulfide has formed?

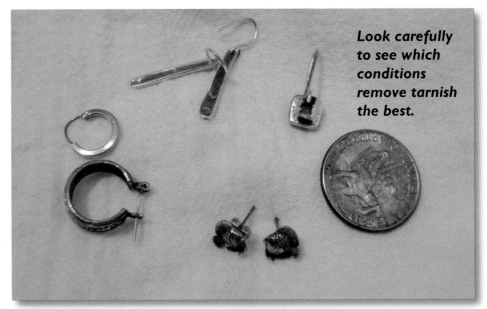

Look carefully to see which conditions remove tarnish the best.

METAL PLATING

An extremely useful form of reduction is metal plating. In this process, metal ions move from one object to another. A metal source, such as zinc or copper, sheds metal cations into solution. The cations form a coat on a metal object to give its surface new properties. A new metal coat can make a pan heat faster or a ring shinier. In most industrial plating, an electric current makes the plating process more efficient. However, galvanized steel, an extremely durable material, is made without the electric current; instead the steel is dipped in a hot zinc bath.

Try your hand at dip plating with an iron nail or a brass key and supplies you probably already have at home. Coins make an excellent source of metal for plating. The tiny amounts of metal that the coins give off will not damage them.

MATERIALS

- 2 nails or brass keys
- dish soap
- scrub brush or old toothbrush
- 20 copper pennies (U.S. dates of 1981 and before)
- 20 zinc pennies (U.S. dates of 1983 and later)
- kitchen towel
- digital camera
- 2 glass jars
- marker
- vinegar
- measuring cup
- salt
- tongs or tweezers

INSTRUCTIONS

1. Scrub the iron nails or brass keys thoroughly with a brush and dish soap until they are completely free of grime. Rinse thoroughly.
2. Lay the nails or keys next to one of each kind of penny on a clean kitchen towel and take pictures of the objects with the digital camera.
3. Label one glass jar COPPER; label the second ZINC. Add ¼ cup vinegar to each glass jar. Drop the 20 copper pennies in the COPPER jar and the 20 zinc pennies in the ZINC jar. Let the pennies sit, undisturbed, for at least 3 minutes. During this time, copper or zinc ions will move out of the pennies and into solution.
4. Drop one cleaned iron nail or brass key from step 1 into each jar. Let the reaction proceed for at least 15 minutes. Watch and take notes. What is happening to the nail and key? To the pennies?
5. Use tongs or tweezers to carefully remove the plated object and one penny from each jar. Set them on a clean towel. Take pictures of the plated objects and the pennies. Compare your "before plating" (from step 2) and "after plating" pictures.

Take it further: Not all metal sources plate as well as copper and zinc. What happens if you use other sources of metal to plate a nail or key, such as silver quarters (mint dates 1932–1964), aluminum foil, metal pipes, metal wire, or door hinges? (The best results will come from objects of pure copper, such as copper wire or copper pipes.)

MAKE YOUR OWN PLASTIC

The term *plastic* in chemistry refers to chemical units that react with each other to form long chains, like paper clips can, or like chain-link fences. Plastics are strong and durable because they are the same throughout, and they tend not to react easily with other chemicals.

Most of today's plastics are made from petroleum compounds. These products are extremely strong and durable. The downside is that they do not break down well once they are thrown away. Experts estimate that plastic grocery store bags, made from polyethylene, may not break down in landfills for over 500 years. New **biodegradable** plastics are being invented, such as those made from corn oil. These new plastics are not too different from natural plastics people learned to make at home long ago from plant or animal material. You can create your own durable, biodegradable plastic using milk.

Plastic has given us some amazing toys over the years!

MATERIALS

- whole milk
- nonstick pot
- candy thermometer
- vinegar
- stove
- **an adult**
- cheesecloth
- colander
- mixing bowl
- bowls, hardened clay, or other molding surfaces

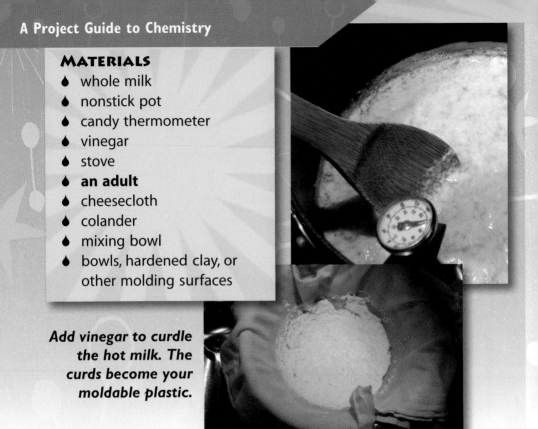

Add vinegar to curdle the hot milk. The curds become your moldable plastic.

INSTRUCTIONS

1. Before you begin, think about what you want to make with your final product. A small toy? A vase for your mom? A bowl for your cereal? One cup of milk will yield enough food-safe plastic to make a hockey puck. Use more milk to make larger objects.
2. Measure the milk in 1-cup increments and add it to a nonstick pot. Clip a candy thermometer to the pot and heat the pot over medium-low, stirring occasionally, until the milk reaches 180°F or it begins to foam. With **an adult's** help, remove the pot from the stove.
3. For every 1 cup of milk used, add 1 tablespoon of vinegar to the hot liquid (for 2 cups of milk add 2 tablespoons vinegar, etc.) and stir. The vinegar will cause the milk to separate into chunky curds and liquid whey. The curds are actually long chains of casein, a milk protein, that are too large to stay in solution.
4. Drape a piece of cheesecloth over a colander, and place the colander over a bowl. Ask **the adult** to dump the contents of the pot into the lined colander. Let the curds drain until they are cool enough to touch, about 10 minutes.

After drying for a few days, your milk plastic is ready!

5. Lift the edges of the cheesecloth to make a sack, and squeeze the sack to wring even more whey out of the curds. Place the cheesecloth sack on a clean countertop and open it. Inside, you'll find a lump of white cheese with the texture of crumbly modeling clay.
6. Shape your milk-plastic into whatever you like. At first, the milk plastic will be crumbly and tend to fall apart. You will get the best results if you use a mold. For example, to make a bowl, line the inside of a big bowl with an even, smooth layer of milk plastic, and then nest a smaller bowl inside it. Make molds for toys or statues from modeling clay or florist's foam.
7. Leave the molded plastic out to dry, about one day. Remove the plastic from its mold and let it air-dry completely before using.

Take it further: You can make plastic from Styrofoam packing peanuts, too. Dissolve the packing peanuts in nail polish remover (acetone). Skim the goo off the top of the acetone with a latex-gloved hand and use a mold to shape it into whatever you like. Let the goo dry and harden in the mold for several days to make a lasting plastic object. How does this type of plastic compare to milk plastic?

BREAKING BONDS IN NATURE: PROTEASES

Nature loves to make **polymers** (chains of molecules), especially in living things. Sugars, fats, and proteins are all examples of long chains of repeated units. When it comes to food, however, our body likes it simple. Your stomach and intestines have the important job of breaking down these chains into tiny pieces your body can use. One helper throughout nature is a specialized protein machine that breaks apart protein chains—the protein cannibal! Protein chains are linked by a strong bond that, given enough time, would break down in water. **Proteases** know we can't wait, so they act as a **catalyst**, speeding up the reaction.

Did you know that many tropical fruits make their own proteases? Pineapple and papaya are famous examples. If you've ever eaten raw pineapple and felt your tongue getting rough, that's pineapple's protease—called bromelain—at work. Let's examine the activity of these proteases on gelatin, a yummy protein polymer.

MATERIALS

- **an adult**
- gelatin
- mixing bowl
- 5 small bowls, such as pudding dishes
- fresh pineapple
- 1 can of pineapple
- fresh papaya
- dried papaya
- ruler
- butter knife
- spatula
- marker
- plastic wrap

1. With **an adult**, prepare the gelatin according to package instructions in the mixing bowl. Divide the prepared gelatin evenly into 5 small bowls.
2. Ask **an adult** to help you slice up a fresh pineapple, setting aside a few 1-inch cubes. Thoroughly clean the knife and work area, and then repeat with the fresh papaya. Do the same with the dried papaya, but chop it a little smaller. Be sure not to let papaya juices contaminate the pineapple, and vice versa.
3. Label one bowl CONTROL, cover the gelatin and bowl with plastic wrap, and set it in the refrigerator.
4. For the remaining bowls, add one ingredient each, labeling each bowl accordingly: FRESH PINEAPPLE, CANNED PINEAPPLE, FRESH PAPAYA, DRIED PAPAYA.
5. Cover the bowls with plastic wrap and place them in the refrigerator overnight or until set.

6. In the morning, pull all five bowls out of the refrigerator and set them side by side. Did the gelatin set the same in each bowl? Any proteases in the fruit will have digested some of the protein in the gelatin. Which protease has done the most damage to the gelatin? How do the proteases in fresh fruit compare to those in dried and canned fruit?

Take it further: Experiment to find the best temperature for protease performance. How well do proteases perform at room temperature? How long can they react with the gelatin before their activity dies off? You may also want to test the proteases found in kiwifruit and figs.

Books

Brown, Cynthia Light, and Blair Shedd. *Amazing Kitchen Chemistry Projects You Can Build Yourself.* White River Junction, VT: Nomad Press, 2008.

Gardner, Robert. *Chemistry Science Fair Projects Using Inorganic Stuff.* Berkeley Heights, NJ: Enslow Publishers, 2010.

Gardner, Robert, and Barbara Gardner Conklin. *Organic Chemistry Science Fair Projects.* Berkeley Heights, NJ: Enslow Publishers, 2010.

Greene, Dan. *Chemistry: Getting a Big Reaction.* New York: Kingfisher, 2010.

Newmark, Ann. *Chemistry.* New York: DK Publishing, 2005.

Vecchione, Glen. *100 Amazing Award-Winning Science Fair Projects.* New York: Sterling Publishing Co, Inc., 2005.

Vecchione, Glen. *100 Amazing Make-It-Yourself Science Fair Projects.* New York: Sterling Publishing Co, Inc., 2005.

Winston, Robert. *It's Elementary!* New York: DK Publishing, 2007.

Works Consulted

Brock, William H. *The Norton History of Chemistry.* New York: W.W. Norton & Company, Inc., 1993.

Chang, Raymond. *Chemistry.* New York: McGraw-Hill, Inc., 1994.

Cobb, Cathy, and Harold Goldwhite. *Creations of Fire: Chemistry's Lively History from Alchemy to the Atomic Age.* New York: Plenum Press, 1995.

Gagnon, Steve. "How Do I Make a Model of an Atom?" Jefferson Lab Science Education. http://education.jlab.org/qa/atom_model.html

Hoaglund, Steve. "Additional Experiments." Dutch Neck School Workshop, November 1, 2000. http://www.princeton.edu/~pccm/outreach/scsp/chemtests/tips/hoagland/addexpts.htm

Kiernan, Denise, and Joseph D'Agnese. *Science 101: Chemistry.* Irving, NY: Hydra Publishing, 2007.

Moore, John T. *Chemistry for Dummies.* Hoboken, NJ: Wiley Publishing, Inc., 2003.

Voet, Donald, and Judith G. Voet. *Biochemistry.* Somerset, NJ: John Wiley & Sons, 1995.

On the Internet

American Chemical Society—Science for Kids
http://portal.acs.org/portal/acs/corg/content?_nfpb=true&_
pageLabel=PP_TRANSITIONMAIN&node_id=878&use_sec=false&sec_url_
var=region1&__uuid=5b0318f0-cbb7-44eb-ae96-406ffa11e766

Chemistry—An Introduction
http://www.mcwdn.org/chemist/chemist.html

Chemistry for Kids.net
http://www.chemistryforkids.net/

Rader's Chem 4 Kids
http://www.chem4kids.com/

Science Is Fun in the Lab of Shakhashiri
http://scifun.chem.wisc.edu/

PHOTO CREDITS: Cover, pp. 4, 6, 8, 11, 27, 37, 42—CreativeCommons 2.0; all other photos—Claire O'Neal. Every effort has been made to locate all copyright holders of material used in this book. If any errors or omissions have occurred, corrections will be made in future editions of the book.

acid (AA-sid)—A chemical with a pH less than 7.0.

anion (AN-eye-on)—An atom or group of atoms that has a negative charge.

atom (AA-tum)—The smallest particle that has the chemical properties of an element.

atomic number (uh-TOM-ik NUM-bur)—The number of protons in the nucleus of a given element; this number determines its place in the periodic table.

base—A chemical with a pH greater than 7.0.

biodegradable (BY-oh-dee-GRAY-dih-bul)—Able to break down completely in nature.

bond—Chemical attraction between two atoms in a molecule.

catalyst (KAT-uh-list)—A substance that speeds up a chemical reaction.

cation (KAT-eye-on)—An atom or group of atoms that has a positive charge.

conservation of mass—A physical law stating that matter in the universe cannot be created or destroyed.

dissolve (dih-ZOLV)—To break down in a solution.

electron (ee-LEK-tron)—Any of the tiny, negatively charged particles that orbit the nucleus of an atom.

element (EL-uh-munt)—A chemical compound that contains only one type of atom.

ion (EYE-on)—A charged atom or group of atoms.

isotope (EYE-soh-tohp)—A variety of an element that contains a different number of neutrons than other atoms of the same element.

molecule (MAH-lih-kyool)—A chemical compound made of one or more elements.

neutron (NOO-tron)—A particle in the nucleus with a neutral charge.

nucleus (NOO-klee-us)—The tightly packed core of an atom that contains protons and neutrons.

oxidize (OK-sih-dyz)—To chemically change by removing electrons.

pH (pee-AITCH)—A measurement of the concentration of hydrogen ions in a solution, on a scale of 0 (acidic) to 14 (basic), with pure water measuring 7.0.

polymer (PAH-lih-mer)—A compound formed from small molecules that bond together as a chain.

precipitate (pree-SIH-pih-tut)—A product from a chemical reaction that does not dissolve in the reaction solution.

protease (PROH-tee-ays)—An enzyme that speeds up the chemical breakdown of other proteins.

protein (PROH-teen)—A biological molecule made from amino acids.

proton (PROH-ton)—A positively charged particle in the nucleus of an atom.

radioactive (ray-dee-oh-AK-tiv)—An unstable atom that gives off energy from its nucleus.

reactant (ree-AK-tant)—One of the starting materials in a chemical reaction, listed on the left side of a chemical equation.

reaction (ree-AK-shun)—The process by which the atoms in one or more compounds rearrange to form new compounds.

redox (REE-doks)—A class of reactions that transfer electrons by reduction or oxidation.

reduce (ree-DOOS)—To chemically change by adding electrons.

solution (suh-LOO-shun)—A mixture of completely dissolved substances.

acids 5, 19, 23–26, 30
alkanes 10, 12–13
alkenes 10–11, 12, 13
alkynes 11, 13
antacids 19
Aristotle 4
atomic number 6–7, 8, 9
atoms
    energy in 4, 20
    in chemical equations 14
    in hydrocarbon models 10–13
    parts of 6
    solar system model of 6–9
    theories of 4, 6
balloons 21–22
bases 19, 23–26
biodegradable 37
Bohr, Niels 6
bonds 10
chemical equations 14, 16, 18, 19, 28, 30, 32
coffee filter 17–19, 26
conservation of mass 4, 16
covalent bonds 10
Dalton, John 4
Democritus 4
electrons 5, 6–7, 8, 9, 10, 27, 30, 32, 33, 34
electron shells 6–9
elements 4–5, 6–9, 14
enzymes 5, 42–43
fats 10, 40
fire 4, 27–29
hydrocarbons 5, 10–13
hydrogen 4, 7, 10–13, 15, 23

ions 23, 34, 35, 36
    anions 15
    cations 15, 30, 35
isotopes 9
Lavoisier, Antoine 4
mass number 7–9
Mayow, John 27, 28–29
metal plating 35–36
neutrons 6–7, 8, 9
oxidation 27–30
oxygen 4, 7, 10, 27–30
pennies 35–36
periodic table of the elements 8
pH 23–26
plastics 37–39
polymers 40
precipitates 16, 17–19
Priestley, Joseph 28
proteases 40–43
proteins 5, 10, 38, 40–43
protons 6–7, 8, 9
radioactivity 5
red cabbage indicator 23–25
redox reactions 27–31, 32–34, 35–36
reduction 32–34, 35–36
rust 27, 30–31
safety 5
salts 19
steel wool 30–31
sugars 10, 40
temperature 13, 20–22, 33, 43
turmeric indicator 23, 26
volcano 15
volume 29

A semiretired biochemist, Claire O'Neal has published over a dozen books with Mitchell Lane, including *A Project Guide to Rocks and Minerals, A Project Guide to Earthquakes, A Project Guide to Volcanoes, Exploring Earth's Biomes,* and *Projects in Genetics.* She holds degrees in English and Biology from Indiana University, and a Ph.D. in Chemistry from the University of Washington. She lives in Delaware with her husband, two young sons, and a fat black cat.